Toy Stories 4 Kids

Arriba Up abajo Down at the BOARDWALK
A Book of Opposites
Karl Beckstrand

Includes English/Spanish Español pronunciation guide

THE BRIDGE of the Golden Wood
A Parable on How to Earn a Living
Karl Beckstrand
Y. Cahoua

Crumbs on the Stairs
A Mystery
Karl Beckstrand

WHY JUAN CAN'T SLEEP
A Funny Mystery
Karl Beckstrand Luis F. Sanz

4 Toy Stories for Kids
Multicultural Fun
by Karl Beckstrand
ISBN: 978-1951599508

COUNT toys and animals!

The Bridge of the Golden Wood: A Parable on How to Earn a Living (Careers for Kids series)
Copyright © 2004 Karl Beckstrand, illustrations by Karl Beckstrand & Yaniv Cahoua
LCCN: 2016949820, ISBN: 978-1536889864

Why Juan Can't Sleep: A Funny Mystery
Text Copyright © 2010 Karl Beckstrand, illustration copyright © 2012 Luis F. Sanz
LCCN: 2012914948, ISBN: 978-0615692296

Crumbs on the Stairs: A Mystery (Mini-Mysteries for Minors)
Text and illustration Copyright © 2007 Karl Beckstrand
 ISBN: 978-0977606535

Arriba Up, Abajo Down at the Boardwalk (Sports Books for Kids)
Text and illustration Copyright © 2012 Karl Beckstrand
LCCN: 2012912901, ISBN: 978-0615688237

Premio Publishing & Gozo Books   Hurricane, UT, USA
© 2025. All rights reserved. This book, or parts thereof, may not be reproduced or shared in any form—except by reviewer, who may quote brief passages or sample illustrations in a printed, online, or broadcast review—without prior written permission from the publisher. Derechos reservados. Queda prohibida la reproducción o transmisión de parte alguna de esta obra, sin permiso escrito del publicador.

ORDER direct, or via major book distributors

FREE ebooks, lesson plans, exclusive book bundles, and online SECRETS:

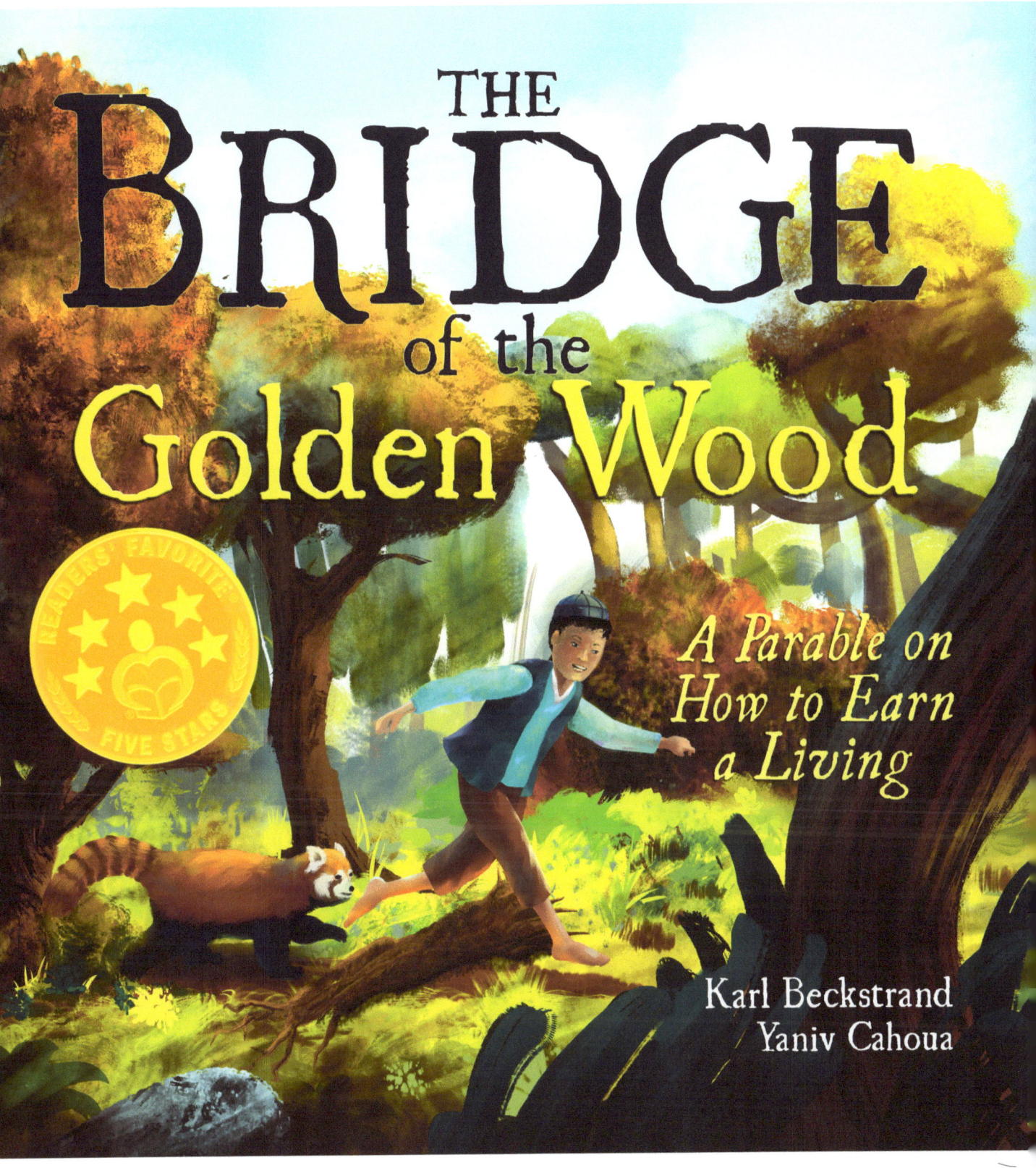

The Bridge of the Golden Wood

Premio Publishing & Gozo Books
Hurricane, UT, USA
Library of Congress Control Number: 2016949820
ISBN: 978-1536889864
ASIN: B01N0XCPQK
Illustrations by Yaniv Cahoua & Karl Beckstrand
Book 4 in **Careers for Kids** series; Copyright © 2017 Karl Beckstrand

For Dad, who never feared work but also took time to play

All rights reserved: This book, or parts thereof, may not be reproduced or shared in any form—except by reviewer, who may quote brief passages or sample illustrations in a printed, online, or broadcast review—without prior written permission from the publisher. Derechos reservados. Queda prohibida la reproducción o transmisión de parte alguna de esta obra, sin permiso escrito del publicador. Nothing herein is intended as legal or investment advice.

Other books/ebooks by Karl Beckstrand:
Agnes's Rescue, Ida's Witness, Anna's Prayer, Samuel Sailing (nonfiction)
She Doesn't Want the Worms! – ¡Ella no quiere los gusanos!
Crumbs on the Stairs – Migas en las escaleras: A Mystery
No Offense: Communication Guaranteed Not to Offend
Sounds in the House – Sonidos en la casa: A Mystery
The Dancing Flamingos of Lake Chimichanga
GROW! How We Get Food from Our Garden
Horse & Dog Adventures in Early California
Bright Star, Night Star: An Astronomy Story
Polar Bear Bowler: A Story Without Words
Arriba Up, Abajo Down at the Boardwalk
Bad Bananas: A Story Cookbook for Kids
Butterfly Blink: A Book Without Words
Gopher Golf: A Wordless Picture Book
Why Juan Can't Sleep: A Mystery?
Ma MacDonald Flees the Farm

ORDER direct, or via major distributors. Libros online books FREE/GRATIS

KidsWorldBooks.com

There once was a boy who loved to make things. He was always finding better ways to do things. He could even create useful things from objects that others saw as useless.

He always carried tools with him—and he usually had a rope nearby (it was handy for swinging, hauling, and securing things).

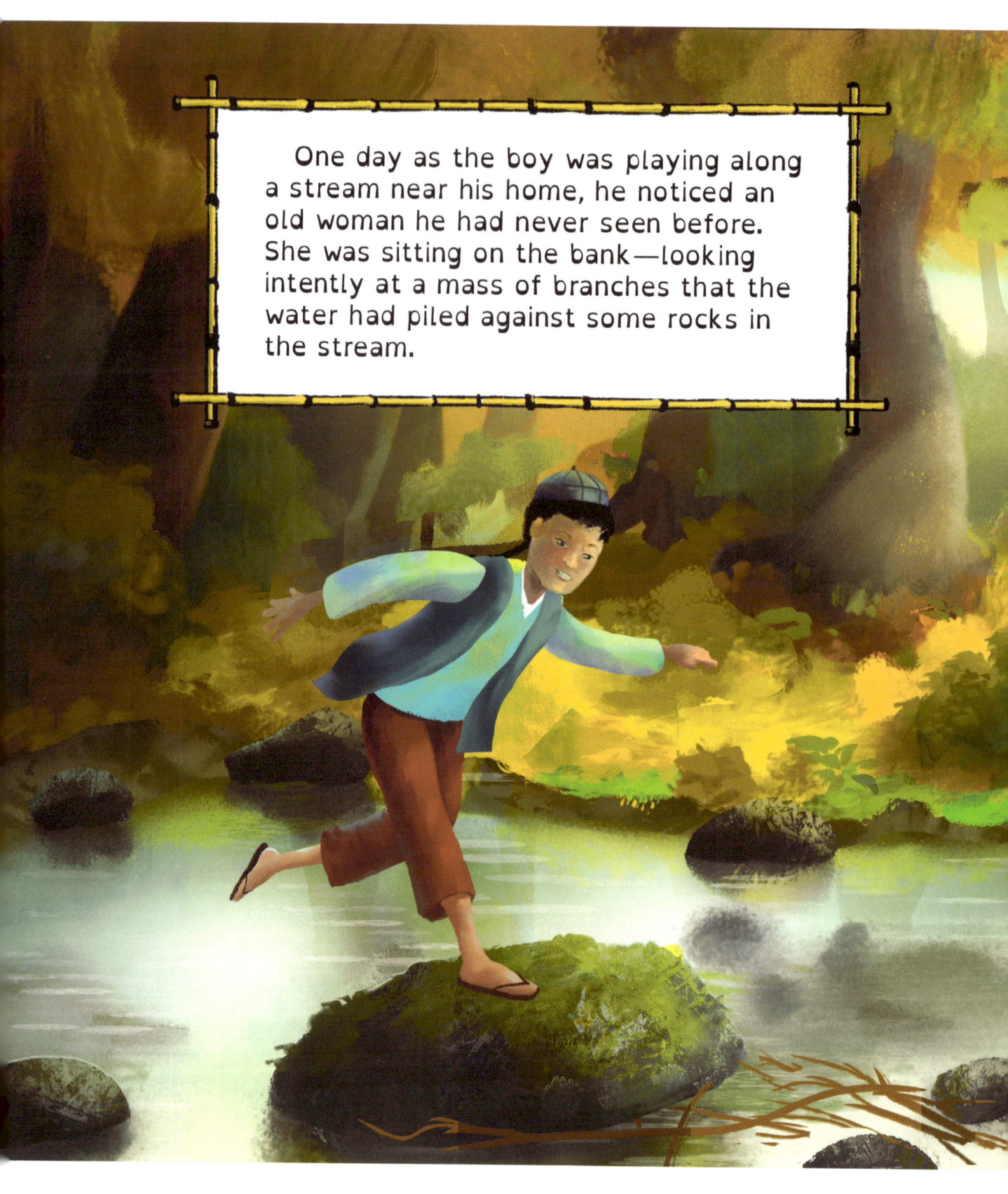

One day as the boy was playing along a stream near his home, he noticed an old woman he had never seen before. She was sitting on the bank—looking intently at a mass of branches that the water had piled against some rocks in the stream.

"Hello," said the boy, curious to know who she was—and why she stared so intently at the dead wood.

"Hello," said the old woman, not taking her eyes from the branches.

"What are you looking at?" asked the boy.

"Trouble and treasure," she said.

"Treasure?" asked the boy.
"That wood is as valuable as gold," she said. "But it is blocking the path of the fish, who must feed beyond it down the stream. For them it is trouble." Then she looked at the boy for the first time. "Will you help?"
"Well, I..."
"If you do, you will have the treasure."

The clever boy needed no more encouragement. He already had a plan. He quickly climbed a tree to retrieve his swinging rope.

The old woman smiled as the boy sat on the bank and took off his shoes. "Excuse, me," he said, turning back to the woman. "How will I know when I've found the treas..."
There was no one there—only a splash in the water and the tailfin of a fish going under it.

The boy looked around and peered into the nearby bushes. "Well," he said, rolling up his sleeves, "at least I can help the fish get to their food." The boy waded into the stream and began to gather the branches and lift them on top of the rocks they were pinned against. He was able to wrap his rope under and over them until they were in a large, tidy bundle supported by the rocks that had once trapped them.

As he tied some knots, he noticed eager fish swimming around and past him under his bundle of branches.

Just as the boy was leaving the water, a man with a large sack on his back approached the stream. "I'll give you a gold coin," he said, "if you let me across your bridge."

"My bridge?" said the boy. "Ah, of course! Please come across." The man thanked him and gave him a small coin of gold before going on his way.

Every day after that many travelers and peddlers came across the boy's bridge, and each of them gave the boy gold (which his parents let him keep, since his idea and effort had created the source of the income).

The boy spent many a happy day playing along the stream, watching the fish feed, and earning money to feed his family. He never saw the old woman again.

What did the boy do that helped him to find the treasure? How might you find treasure in trouble?
Problems and needs are opportunities to help and can lead to income. See opportunity in every obstacle. Can you solve problems or serve people? Then you can earn money—even pay for your living expenses and those of others. What if you see a need, fill it, but don't get paid? Are you sure you weren't paid? How do you feel helping someone? Pretty good, huh? (Some people pay with things or via service.) Even without pay, you gain a reputation as a worker, a problem solver—plus you get experience to make you more valuable to future customers (you may also get ideas for products/services that could earn money in the future). Some ideas below may not be suitable for where you live or for someone your age; be sure to have an adult go over your plans before you begin a project (also see local and country business laws). The only guarantee of success is what you guarantee yourself through your imagination, effort, and persistence.

EARNING IDEAS

Make something to sell.
Clean, fix, or repurpose something.
Collect something to sell.
Create something to sell.
Grow/raise something to sell.
Recycle for cash.
Rent things to people who need them.
Trade things for something more valuable to you.
Sell/give something extra you can spare.
Sell other people's product to earn a percentage.
Perform/entertain.
Publish a book/ebook, then...
Research & share information.
Participate/share your opinion for a reward.
Transport things for compensation.

EXAMPLES

Cupcakes, an app, a shoe rack, soap, kites
Bicycles, windows, furniture, appliances, tools
Stamps, coins, books, games, antiques, wood, fruit
Photographs, paintings, music, fonts, games, crafts
Watermelon, lavender, nuts, sheep, pets
Metal, glass, plastic, electronics, paper, clothes
Property, tools, vehicles, ad space, electronics
Toys for games, electronics, clothes, or collectibles
Books, toys, games, clothes, gadgets
Candles, cookies, apps, magazines, ad space
Sing/dance/act/play a musical instrument, do magic
Teach classes, speak to groups, write a blog or a newsletter, share information via video/audio/Web
Surveys, polls, focus groups, studies, mystery shop
Pets, people, recyclables, junk, wood, garbage cans

WORK FOR SOMEONE ELSE

Work for a friend, family member, or company—or provide a specific service to many people/clients as a contractor (some work requires a license and/or permits).

As you get older and wiser, your opportunities to earn money increase. There is ALWAYS work to be found or something that needs fixing/improving. Perhaps the only job you see is not the kind of work you prefer; consider taking it for the experience and to network (meet new people and learn of other opportunities).

START A BUSINESS OR FRANCHISE

Solve a problem/provide goods or services that meet people's needs. Seek expert input. Get a business license and tax ID.

- For best results, continue to study business, computers, spelling, grammar, math, speaking, marketing, business law—and the industries that interest you.
- Never sell something that isn't yours unless you have permission from the owners to do so (even art and ideas).
- As your business grows, hire a team of hardworking people (especially those with skills you don't possess).
- Always plan your work; write specific goals and steps! Be flexible and creative. Make house calls. Work. Do your best. Be helpful—even if there seems to be no reward. Find partners with integrity. Budget your time and money. Keep your word. Be positive. Make decisions based on the best facts available (know your industry!). Constantly improve. Take care of your health. Be honest. Be Kind.

EXAMPLES

Paper route, walk/groom pets, run errands, child care, wash & detail cars, clean houses, move furniture, chop wood, repair bikes. Some things—like mowing lawns/landscaping, raking leaves, or shoveling snow—are seasonal and can replace other seasonal activities.

TIP: If a company you want to work for isn't hiring, consider volunteering your time. This way, you will gain experience and the company will see what a good worker you can be.

EXAMPLES

Build web sites, sell products or services online, review/rate organizations, clean homes/offices, build things/buildings, promote other people's products/services, connect like-minded people (create an association/newsletter/conference), invent a life-simplifying product, create an app that tracks spending or caloric intake or gives other information, repair electronics/appliances/vehicles/furniture, transport people/things, teach other people to do something that you have done.

TIP: Be sure you can trust the people you work for and with. Signed agreements can help you avoid some conflicts.

TIP: Education can make a great difference in your earnings; it doesn't have to be a college degree; consider trade schools, self study, and apprenticeships. Some companies will train you. (Travel is a great education too!) Each person has gifts that need to be discovered to help others and self. With practice, something you thought you were bad at may become your greatest ability.

SEE: ChildrenEarn.com for information on finding customers, managing money, and moving up in an organization. **Like this book?** *Please comment online!* **More Careers for Kids books:** *Great Cape o' Colors - Capa de colores; Bright Star, Night Star: An Astronomy Story; Ma MacDonald Flees the Farm: It's Not a Pretty Picture...Book*

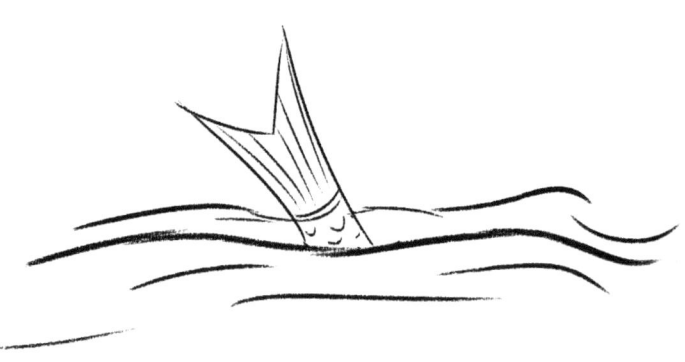

WHY JUAN CAN'T SLEEP

A Funny Mystery

Karl Beckstrand Luis F. Sanz

Why Juan Can't Sleep: A Mystery?

Premio Publishing & Gozo Books
Midvale, UT, USA
Library of Congress Catalog No.: 2012914948

Text Copyright © 2012 Karl Beckstrand
Illustration Copyright © 2012 Luis F. Sanz

All rights reserved: This book, or parts thereof, may not be reproduced or shared in any form—except by reviewer, who may quote brief passages or sample illustrations in a printed, online, or broadcast review—without prior written permission from the publisher. Derechos reservados. Queda prohibida la reproducción o transmisión de esta obra, sin permiso escrito del publicador.

FIND the bear, lamb, camel, dragon, dog, crickets, mosquito, cat, bird, and rabbit.

 KidsWorldBooks.com

Crazy day
—of work and play—
worn-out Juan

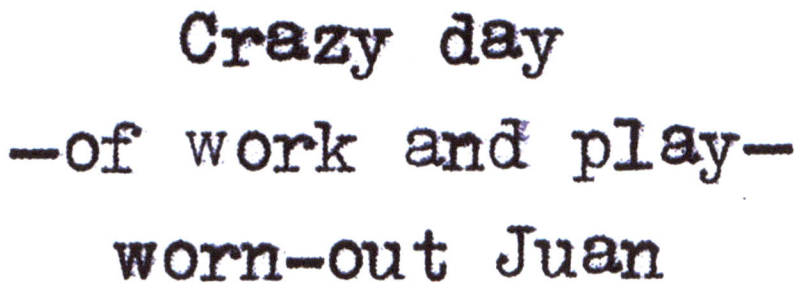

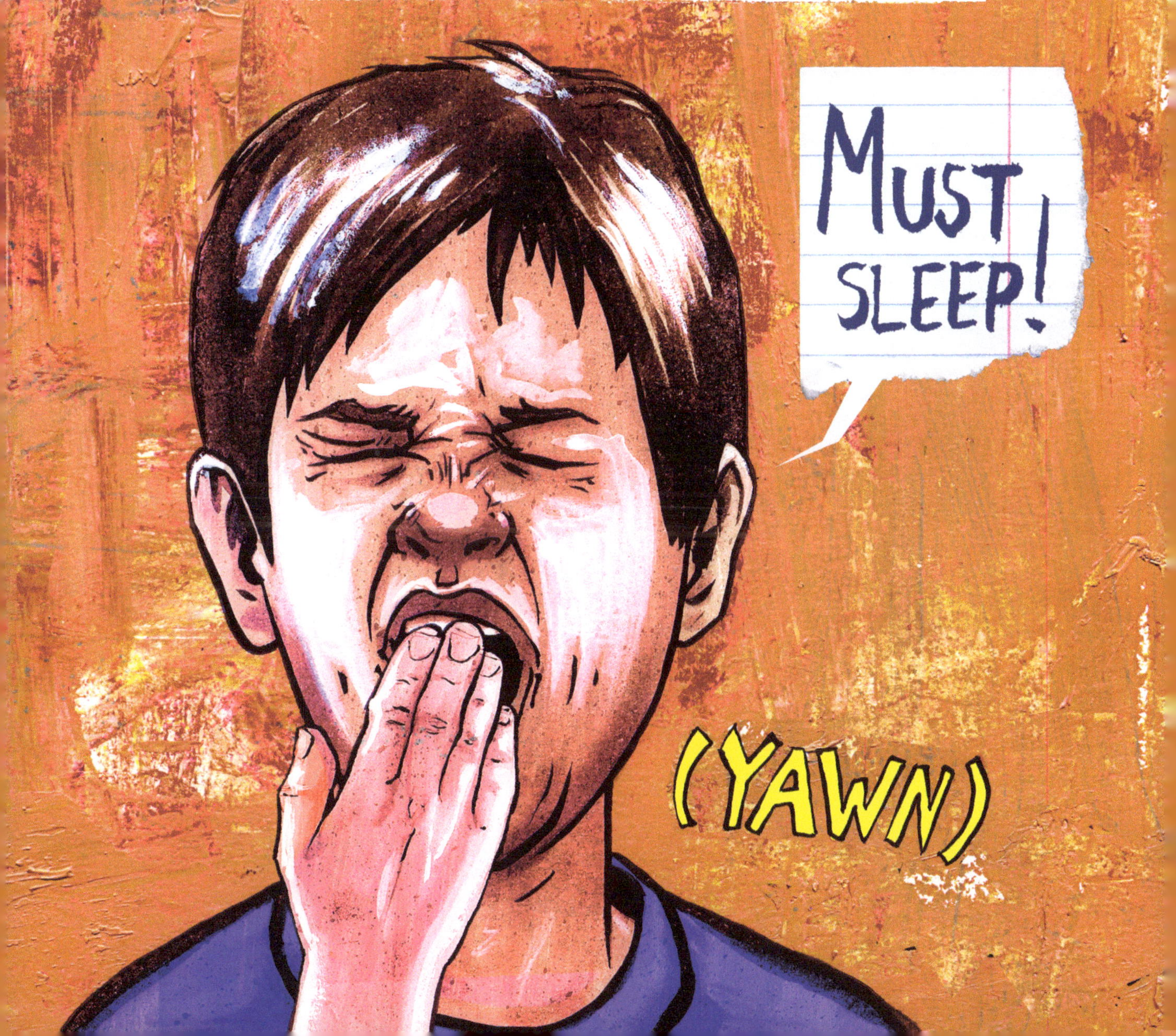

Tonight he won't be
counting lambies.
poop-ed-ness fills the air.

Instead he dreams of driving with Grandpa.

Crickets croon.
The floor creaks.

[Crumbs are in my shirt!]

A sound from the ground...

Punching his pillow, Juan settles again.

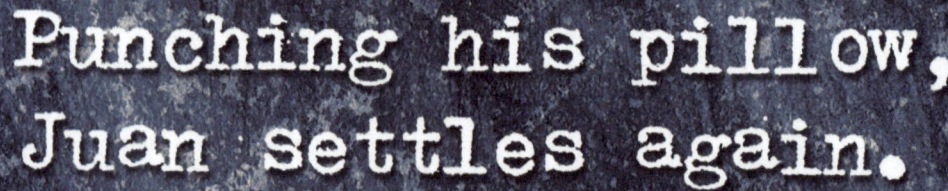

...AND THE NUMBER ONE THING THAT KEEPS PEOPLE UP AT NIGHT IS...

Itches... twitches; he picks at his stitches. He thinks about riches.

he's dreaming of
WITCHES!

A plane, a train, thunder and rain, police in the lane...

Urp! Last night's lo mein.

He counts in his brain,

The strain, the pain!

(he's bursting a vein)
—He's going insane.

There's a ghost in the glow!

NO, A DANCE OF THE PANTS

dragging,
droopy,
... dreamland?

Crumbs on the Stairs

A Mystery

Written & illustrated by
Karl Beckstrand

For Gregory and Hysen

This book available in Spanish-only, bilingual, & ebook versions: Premiobooks.

Aunque se escriben diferente, todas las palabras que encuentres en inglés en este libro y que terminen en -ear, -ere, -air(s), -are(s), y -aire tienen el mismo sonido al terminar: -er. En inglés, la H no es muda; se pronuncia como la J de español. *Crumbs* se pronuncia: *kramz*.

Crumbs on the Stairs

Premio Publishing & Gozo Books, LLC
Midvale, UT, U.S.A.
Text and illustrations copyright ©2011 Karl Beckstrand
First printing 2007
ISBN: 978-0-9776065-3-5

All rights reserved. This book, or parts thereof, may not be reproduced or transmitted in any form—except by reviewer, who may quote brief passages or sample illustrations in a printed, online, or broadcast review—without prior written permission from the publisher.

Images of Linda Ronstadt and the Mamas & the Papas used with permission

Other books by Karl Beckstrand: *Sounds in the House, Anna's Prayer* (Leatherwood Press)
BAD Bananas – A Story Cookbook for Kids, She Doesn't Want the Worms - Ella no quiere los gusanos

Discounts available for fundraising, bulk, school, and charitable donation orders

Premio Publishing
& Gozo Books, LLC

mini mysteries for
for minors (2 - 8)

Count the bear!

Would you care to compare where the bear makes his lair? (Count him!)

...on the bear...

And if you were to stare at your fair cousin, Claire, what would you find in her hair?

Now,
Javier would swear
—if you asked
(with a glare)
just why
there are
crumbs...

...on the bear, and the chair, and the hair of your fair cousin, Claire...

Crumbs!

WHERE did all the crumbs come from?

WHY are there crumbs on the stairs?

WHO is dropping crumbs everywhere?

Find out inside!

Premiobooks.

Premio Publishing & Gozo Books, LLC

mini mysteries for minors (2 - 8)

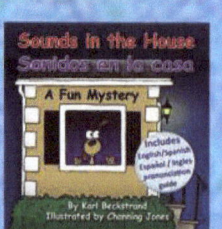
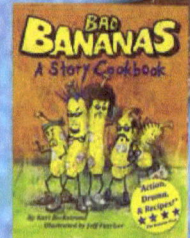

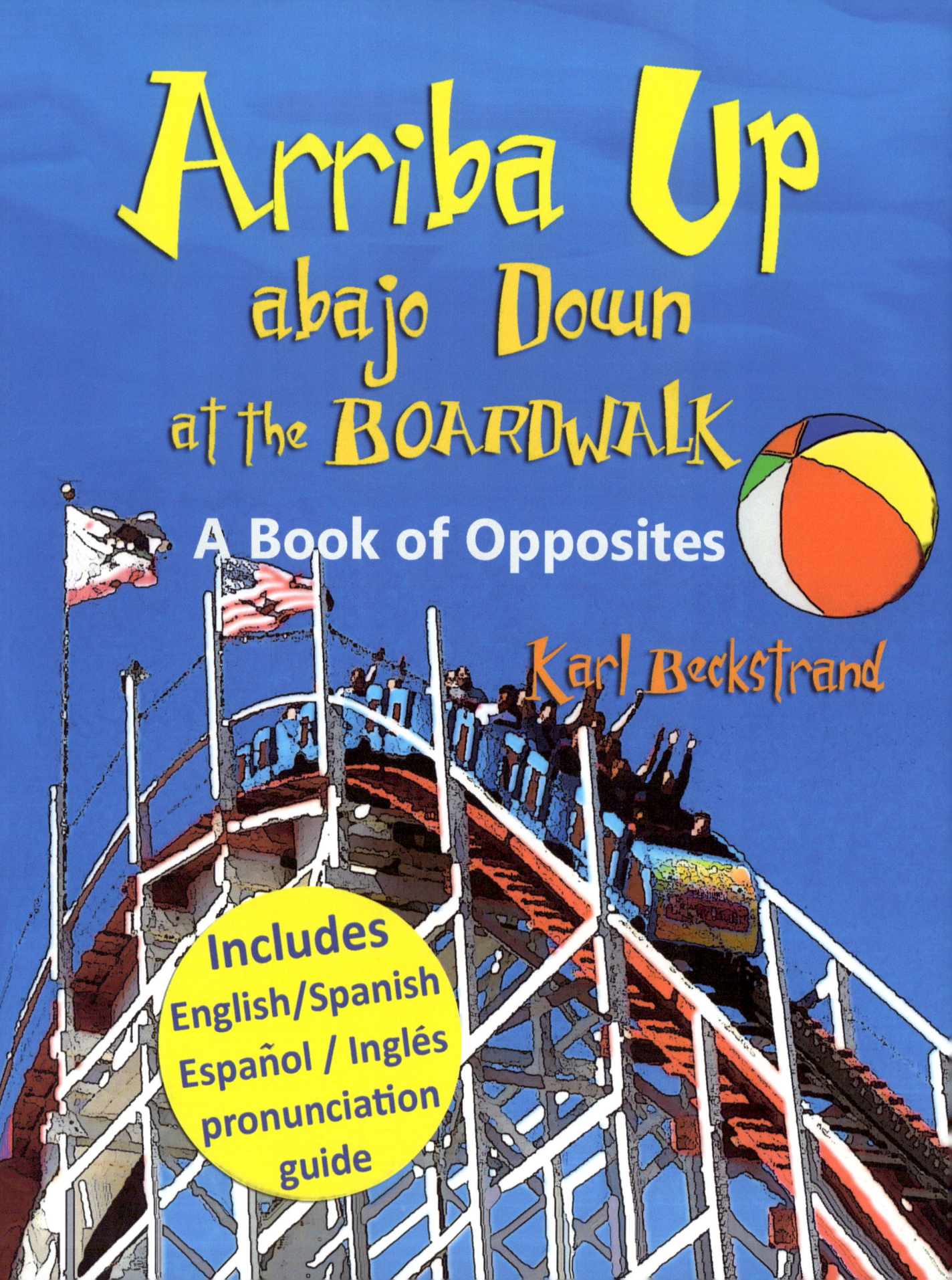

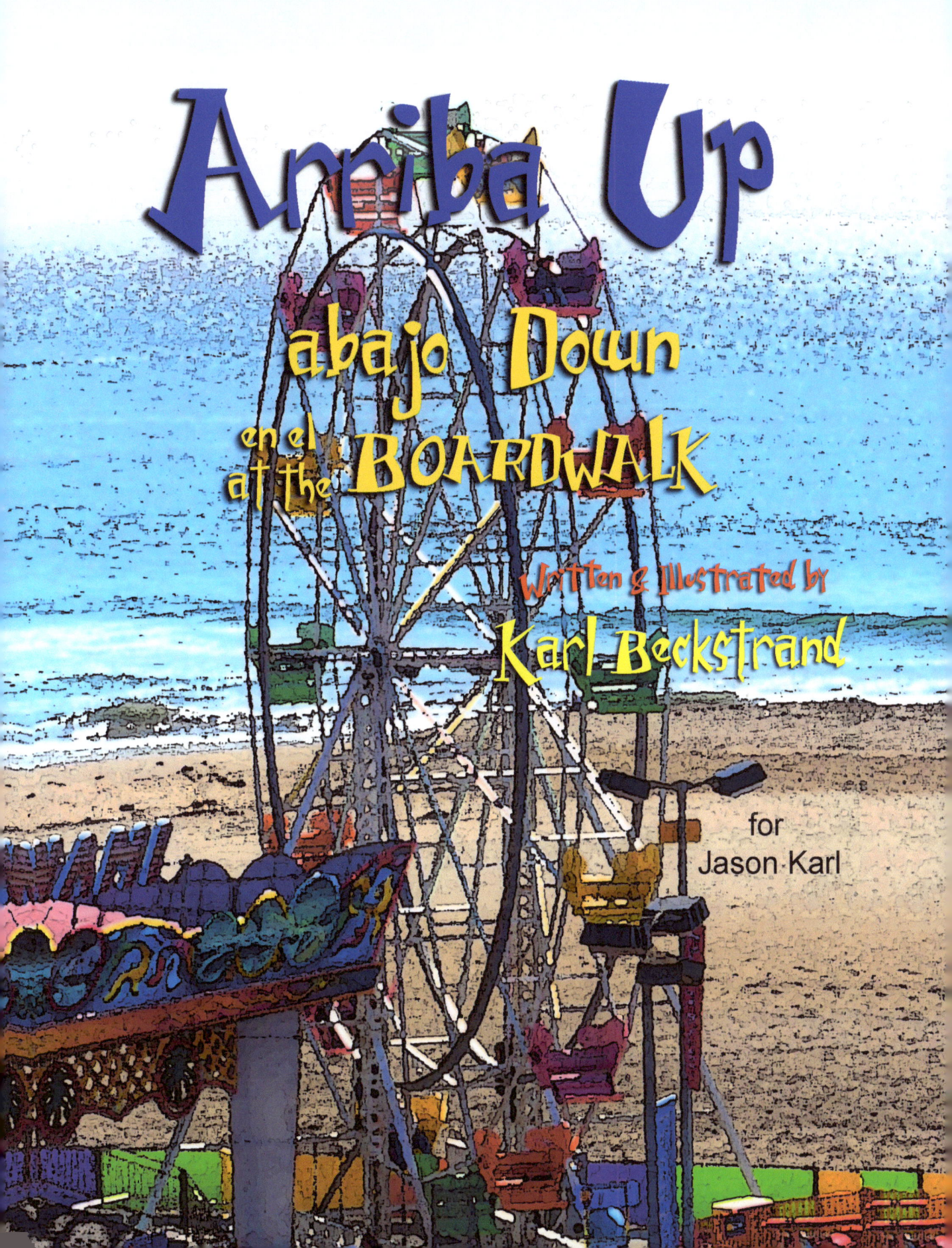

Arriba Up, abajo Down at the Boardwalk
A Book of Opposites in English & Spanish
This book is available in English-only, Spanish-only, and e-book versions:
Premiobooks.com

Spanish vowels have one sound each: a = ah e = eh i = ee o = oh u = oo. Every vowel should be pronounced (except for the u after a q). In Spanish, the letter j is pronounced as an English h (and the letter h is silent), ll sounds like a y (or a j in some countries), and ñ has an ny sound (año sounds like ah-nyo).

Aunque se escriben diferente, todas las palabras que encuentres en inglés en este libro que terminen en -oun u -own tienen el mismo sonido al terminar: "aun" (-ouns y -owns se pronuncian "auns", -ound u -ownd: "aund", -ounds u -ownds: "aunds"). En inglés el d tiene un sonido más fuerte (similar al t de tomar) y la h se pronuncia como la j de español. "Up" se pronuncia "Ap".

Special thanks to the historic Santa Cruz Beach Boardwalk in California for use of original images

Premio Publishing & Gozo Books, LLC
Midvale, UT, USA
Library of Congress Catalog Number: 2012912901
ISBN: 978-0615688237
eISBN: 978-1452476285
Illustration & Text Copyright © 2012 Karl Beckstrand

All rights reserved: This book, or parts thereof, may not be reproduced in any form--except by reviewer, who may quote brief passages or sample illustrations in a printed, online, or broadcast review--without prior written permission from the publisher. Derechos reservados. Queda prohibida la reproducción o transmisión de esta obra, sin permiso escrito del publicador.

Available in English, Spanish, and ebook
Premiobooks.com and major distributors

Libros Online books FREE/GRATIS:
Premiobooks.com

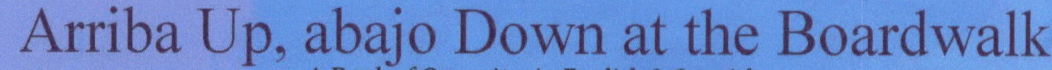

Arriba
Up

(Count the ball.)
(Cuenta las pelotas.)

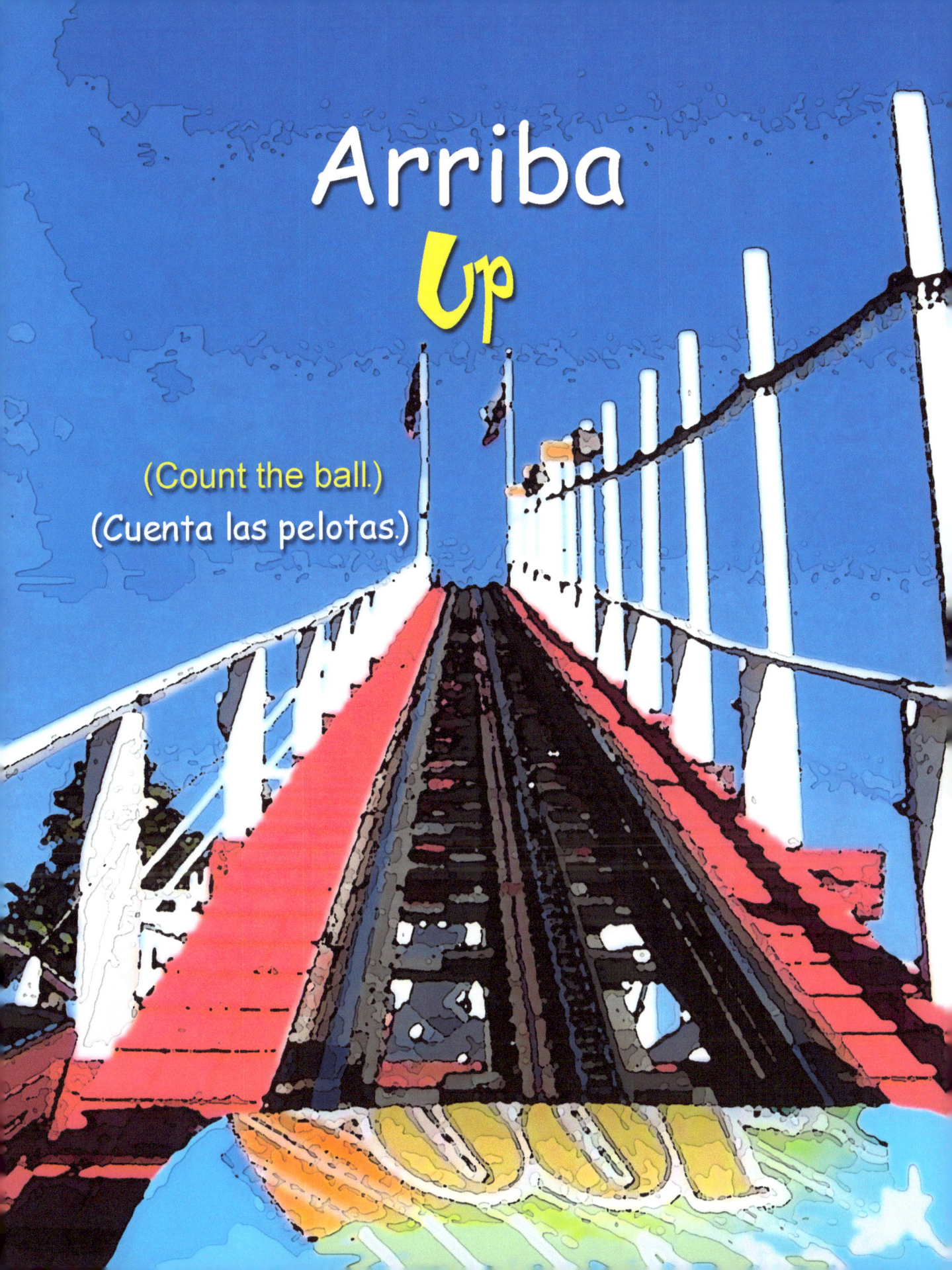

smile

sonrisa

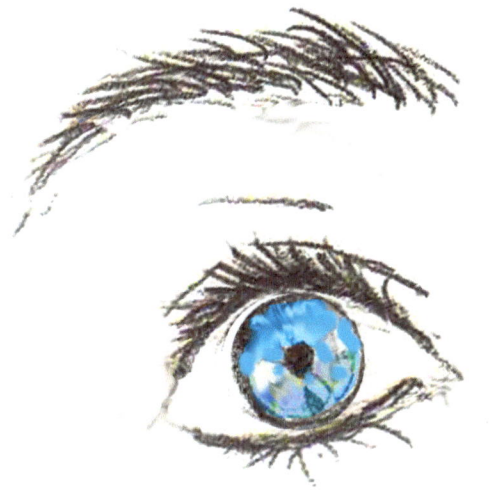

frown

disgusto

hoyo y montículo
pit and mound

brinco y salto
leap and bound

www.ingramcontent.com/pod-product-compliance
Lightning Source LLC
Chambersburg PA
CBHW041545220426
43665CB00002B/37